Discover India
State by State

OFF TO TRIPURA

SONIA MEHTA

PUFFIN BOOKS

An imprint of Penguin Random House

PUFFIN BOOKS

USA | Canada | UK | Ireland | Australia | New Zealand | India | South Africa | China | Singapore

Puffin Books is part of the Penguin Random House group of companies whose addresses can be found at global.penguinrandomhouse.com

Published by Penguin Random House India Pvt. Ltd
4th Floor, Capital Tower 1, MG Road,
Gurugram 122 002, Haryana, India

First published in Puffin Books by Penguin Random House India 2018

Picture Credits

P 12: Tripura Sundari Temple, Udaipur, Tripura (© Bodhisattwa [CC BY-SA 4.0 (https://creativecommons.org/licenses/by-sa/4.0)],
from Wikimedia Commons); P 13: Teliamura, Tripura (© Ashish itct [CC BY-SA 4.0 (https://creativecommons.org/licenses/by-sa/4.0)],
from Wikimedia Commons); P 26: Hozagiri dancers (bijitdutta.com/Shutterstock.com); P 37: Pilak Ruins (© Sanjibroy56 [CC BY-SA 4.0
(https://creativecommons.org/licenses/by-sa/4.0)], from Wikimedia Commons); P 43: A man making cane baskets (Rudra Narayan Mitra/
Shutterstock.com)

The views and opinions expressed in this book are the author's own and the facts are as reported by her, which have been verified to the extent
possible, and the publishers are not in any way liable for the same.

The information in this book is based on research from bona fide sites and published books and is true to the best of the author's knowledge at
the time of going to print. The author is not responsible for any further changes or developments occurring post the publication of this book.
This series is not a comprehensive representation of the states of India but is intended to give children a flavour of the lifestyles and cultures of
different states. All illustrations are artistic representations only.

ISBN 9780143441014

Design and layout by Quadrum Solutions Pvt. Ltd
Printed at Repro India Limited

www.penguin.co.in

This is a legitimate digitally printed version of the book and therefore might not
have certain extra finishing on the cover.

Hello Kids!

I'm so happy you are reading this book. India is an incredible country and there are lots of things about it that we never get to hear about.

I discovered India because my father was in the Indian army. He was posted to many places all over India—and we dutifully followed him. Can you imagine that by the time I was in the tenth standard, I had changed nine schools? Of course it was hard making new friends almost every year, but the good part was that I got to live in so many places. Right from Kerala, where I was born, to Kashmir, Jhansi, Shillong, Chandigarh, Goa . . . the list is long.

Every time I go to a new place, I feel amazed at how different each state is from the other—and yet, how similar. Did you know that we can see monuments from the Stone Age right here in India? Or that we have more than twenty official languages, and most Indians know three or four on an average? Or even that some of the world's most amazing scientific marvels were invented in India?

Oh, there are many, many, many fun and fantastic things about the states of India, which we simply must get to know.

So get your backpack ready, get set to meet some new friends and join me on a fun trip as we **DISCOVER INDIA, STATE BY STATE**.

I hope you enjoy reading this book as much as I have enjoyed writing it. I would love to hear from you. So do write to me at sonia.mehta@quadrumltd.com.

Lots of love,
Sonia Aunty

Mishki and Pushka have come to visit Earth from their home planet, Zoomba. They have never seen such an amazing place. Zoomba doesn't have trees and mountains and rivers like Earth does. But the people look exactly the same. When they come to Earth, they meet a sweet old man whom they call Daadu Dolma. Daadu Dolma shows them all the wonderful places in India and tells Mishki and Pushka all about them.

Mishki and Pushka can't believe what they see. They have seen a lot of Earth, but they have never, ever seen a place like India.

They are off to explore India state by state :)

Mishki

Mishki is a curious little girl. She is always asking loads of questions. On her home planet, she is always getting into trouble for poking her nose into things that are not her business.

Pushka

Pushka is Mishki's brother. He **loves adventure**. He is always ready for a new challenge. Whether it's climbing a mountain, or diving into a cold, cold sea, he is up for it.

Daadu Dolma

Daadu Dolma is a wise old man who has lived on Earth longer than the mountains and the seas. No one knows quite how old he is, but he certainly has been around. He knows everything about everything.

Mishki has finished packing and is waiting patiently for Pushka and Daadu.

'Daadu,' she says, 'I know Tripura is somewhere in the north of India. Does that mean it is super cold?'

'Tripura is in the north-east of India. So it doesn't have the freezing climate of the Himalayas,' replies Daadu. 'But if you want to know what's really special about it, I'd say its culture.'

'I bet the food is great too,' adds Pushka.

Daadu laughs. Pushka is always hungry.

'There are many things that are terrific about Tripura, but if we don't leave now, we'll never find out,' he says. 'Are you ready to go?'

'YES!' shout Mishki and Pushka together. They are

OFF TO TRIPURA!!!

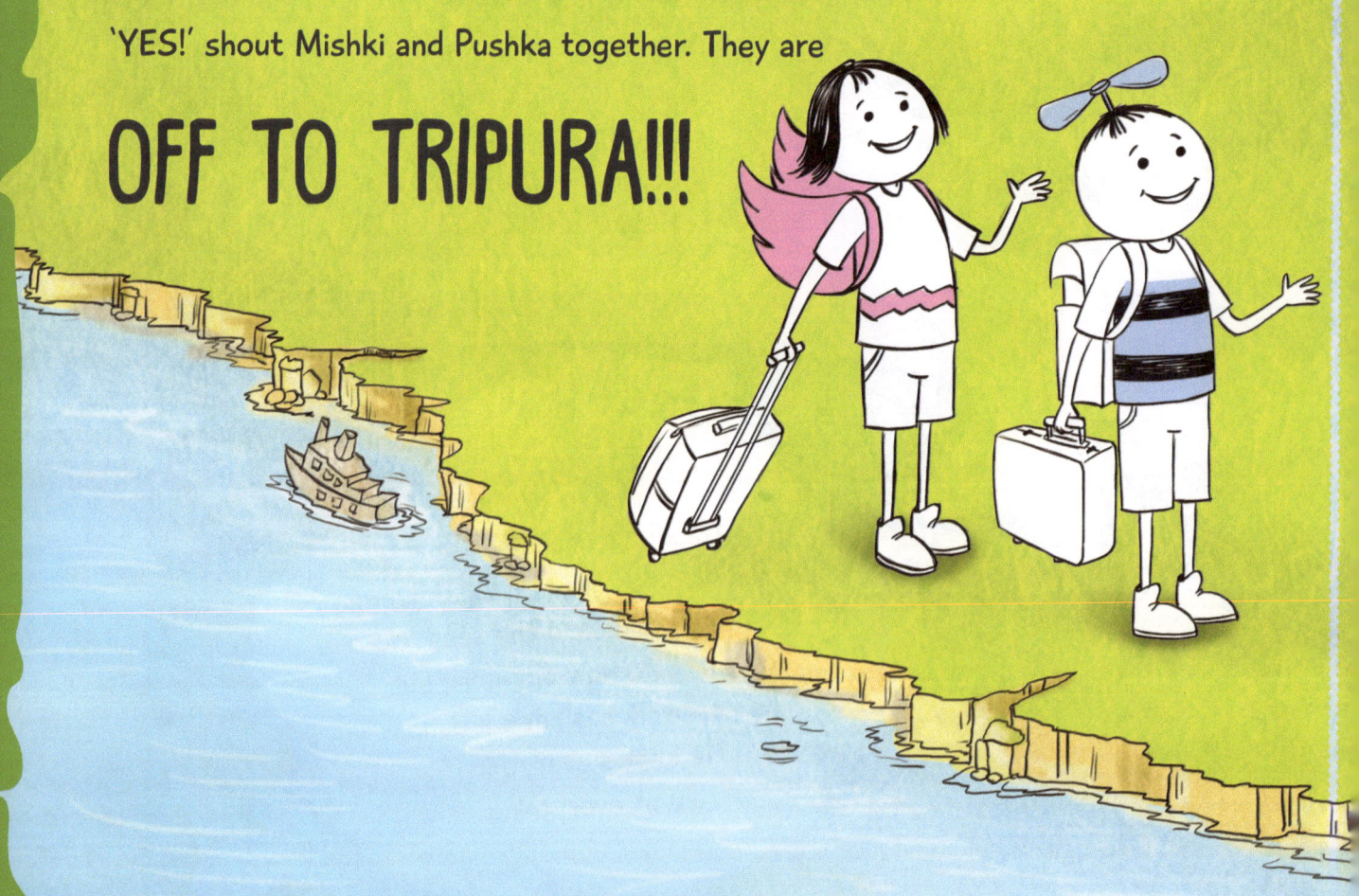

Land ahoy!

It certainly does! This tiny state has some spectacular hills, valleys and rivers, making it a very lovely place to visit.

Wow! Tripura seems to have a lot of natural beauty. Look at the shades of green!

ON THE MAP

To see exactly where **Tripura** is on the map of India, go to

http://www.mapsofindia.com/maps/india/india-political-map.htm

A HAPPY LITTLE NEIGHBOURHOOD

If you see Tripura on the map of India, it looks like India has its arm protectively around this little state. Tripura has just three neighbours: Bangladesh, Mizoram and Nepal. It's one of India's tiniest states.

Tripura is one of seven states in India's north-east known as the Seven Sisters. Its other sisters are Nagaland, Assam, Meghalaya, Mizoram, Manipur and Arunachal Pradesh.

HILLY BILLY

A large part of Tripura is hilly terrain. There are four major valleys that criss-cross these hills: the Dharmanagar, the Kailashahar, the Kamalpur and the Khotwai valleys. The hills rise to meet small mountain ranges named the Sakhan Tlang range, the Langtarai range, the Athara Mura range and the Deota Mura range.

VALLEYS AND PLAINS

All of Tripura isn't hilly. There are marshy valleys in the lower reaches. And there is the massive Agartala plain, which extends from the Ganga and Brahmaputra basins. This area is great for farmers.

RIVER RUSH

There are many small and large rivers that meander through the state. The Juri, the Manu, the Deo, the Dhalai and the Khowai are some. The Gumti is one of the larger rivers of this state. It's thanks to these rivers that farming is the main occupation of this state.

WEATHER VANE

Tripura's climate is quite pleasant. The summers can get warm, but nowhere near as hot as in central India. The winters are just cold enough for a shawl or sweater, though the highest parts of the hills and mountains can have some very chilly days. The monsoon, between June and September, brings with it plenty of rain.

FOREST FANTASY

Nearly half of Tripura is covered with forests. There are some lovely trees that grow here. Sal and bamboo are the main trees, and they are super useful to the people who live here.

WILD AND WONDERFUL

With half the state covered with forests, there is plenty of room for wildlife, and you can see some rare animals here. Apart from leopards, tigers, lions and elephants, there are many smaller wild animals too, like jackals, gaurs and gayals. The marshy plains see lots of migratory birds, like storks, ibises and teals, coming here for their annual visit.

LEOPARD SPOTTING

Pushka has spotted a leopard. Can you find its twin?

A

B

C

D

CROP HOP

More than half the people in Tripura are farmers. And half of the state's products are agricultural. The largest crop grown here is rice. There are many cash crops that farmers grow here as well, such as jute, rubber, tea and sugarcane. Oh, and the fruit! Tripura has many orchards of jackfruit, pineapples, oranges and mangoes too! All this must certainly keep farmers busy.

FUN FACTS

State animal
Phayre's langur

State tree
Agar

State bird
Green imperial pigeon

State flower
Nageswar

FARM MAZE

Mishki has decided to work on a farm. But she's already lost in this maze of corn. Can you help her find her way out of it?

CITY CITY BANG BANG

Tripura has some cities that are growing at top speed. They are becoming important places for business and industry. But it also has some tiny, charming towns that still have people living in the old, traditional way.

AGARTALA

This is the capital city of Tripura. The name comes from a perfume tree called agar. *Tala* means storehouse. There is a story about a famous king who tied his elephant to an agar tree, that people believe is still there. Now, Agartala is a fast-growing city with modern buildings and offices.

UDAIPUR

This is different from the Udaipur in Rajasthan. It's most famous for the Tripura Sundari temple that devotees flock to all through the year.

DHARMANAGAR

Blessed by beautiful surroundings, this little city is best known for its scenic beauty. It's considered a great place to live. It has a rich history and many ancient kings are said to have lived here. There are also many historical ruins that are important tourist attractions.

KAILASHAHAR

This city was once the capital of the Tripura kingdom. Close by, you can get to see ruins of monuments from ancient times. Now it's not a very busy place, but tourists make it a point to stop by when they go to see the marvels of the past.

TELIAMURA

This is a tiny little town in the middle of deep forest area. There is a substantial tribal population here. Here's an amazing fact: This city is believed to have among the highest literacy rates in the state of Tripura.

HIDDEN WORDS

AGARTALA isn't that big a name, but you can still make many smaller words from it. Want to try?

AGARTALA

____ ____ ____ ____

____ ____ ____ ____

____ ____

Long, long ago

Daadu, what kind of a history does this state have? Is it very old? Are we going to hear about it?

Right away! We are diving right into Tripura's very interesting past.

AS OLD AS OLD CAN BE

Tripura's history is said to be as old as India's mythology, and that is very old indeed! Some legends say that the name Tripura came from a mighty king called Tripur, who ruled this land much, much before the Mahabharata war. But there are many stories about how Tripura came to be called that.

A LONG JOURNEY INTO INDIA

There are some theories that say a people called the Tipras or the Tipperahs came into central Asia along the same route that the Aryans used—through the Himalayas. They settled down in what is now Allahabad. They called themselves Children of the Water Goddess.

MOVING AROUND

These Tipras weren't able to find a permanent home for themselves. They were ousted from place after place, and they wandered around the northern part of India, looking for somewhere to settle. Some say they wandered through the lower Himalayan region into what today is Assam till they reached a place called Kachhar and finally settled in the region we now call Tripura. This was around 590 CE. They had been wandering for hundreds of years.

Did you know?

The Rajmala is a historical document that says that Tripura was ruled by more than 180 kings for over 5000 years until it became a state.

DYNASTY AFTER DYNASTY

The Rajmala says that one of the dynasties that ruled this region was the Lunar Dynasty. King Druhya married a princess from a small dynasty called Bodo. (This later came to be known as the Bodo tribe.) His parents were not happy and he was disinherited. But not one to be cowed down, Druhya went on a rampage. He defeated the King of Kirata (in the Tripura region) and established his own kingdom. Thereafter, he and his successors ruled for many, many years.

A KING CALLED TRIPUR

More than forty generations later, a boy called Tripur was born in this dynasty. He was said to be a ruthless man. He named his kingdom Tripura. People say that King Tripur was so ruthless that he was eventually killed by none other than Lord Shiva himself!

THE MANIKYA DYNASTY

There are many legends and mythological stories about Tripura's ancient history. But historians begin their own account only in the thirteenth century BCE. According to sources, more than 800 years ago, one of the many kings of Tripura called Ratna Fa gave himself the title of Manikya. Every Tripura maharaja has been called Manikya since.

Some say that Tripura was named after one of Lord Shiva's many names—Tripuresha.

A GOLDEN PERIOD

The Tripura Manikya Dynasty ruled this region for hundreds of years. It was a golden period for Tripura. The regions of Burma (now called Myanmar), Bengal and Assam were all conquered at various times. This was the time that the Mughal empire was spreading in India. But even the Mughals stayed away from the powerful Manikyas.

MANY MANIKYA KINGS

The Manikya kings seemed to have been real visionaries. They did a whole lot of things for their kingdom. They built schools and temples and encouraged business. People were prosperous during their rule, which lasted all the way till Tripura became a separate state.

THE BRITISH ARRIVE!

While the Tripuris (that's what they are called) were happily enjoying life, things were getting rather heated in the rest of India. The British had made India a British colony. They had passed many laws that were unfair to Indians. There were protests and riots all over the country as people insisted that the British leave India and go back to their own country.

PROTECTED BY THE BRITISH

The British had been taking over India region by region. They took control of the Bengal region, which had been a part of the Mughal empire. But Tripura—though a part of this region—was too small for the British to bother much about. They recognized the maharajas of Tripura as the rightful kings, and Tripura became a British protectorate. This meant that the Tripura maharajas accepted the British rule, but they were still allowed to make many of their own laws.

UNREST

Around this time, there were also many fights and struggles among the Tripura royal families for succession to the throne. Whenever it was time for a new king to ascend the throne, royal princes would call on tribal invaders called the Kukis to help them cause unrest, so that they got their way. Finally, the British stepped in. They decided that they would choose the successor whenever a king died.

The Kukis were a collection of hill tribes, who plundered villages and destroyed crops and farms. They also ruthlessly massacred villagers.

INDIA BECOMES INDEPENDENT

The people of India couldn't bear the British rule any more. They were determined to send the British on their way. The riots and protests increased. Many British and Indians were killed and finally, the British decided it was time to leave. They went back to England and in 1947, India became independent from the British rule.

AN INDEPENDENT STATE

After India became independent, the government had to manage the vast country. It was decided that India would be divided into states. Many states were created based on the main language spoken in that region. Tripura, which at this time was a princely state (meaning a state with its own royalty), was merged into the Indian republic. Some years later, it became a union territory. This meant it didn't have its own government like other states did, but was directly under the central government of India. But this didn't satisfy the Tripuris, who had been used to making their own laws for centuries. They protested, and finally in 1972, Tripura became a proper state in its own right.

Talk time

They did! Their languages are influenced by the neighbouring states. Since there are many tribes, there are many dialects that each of them have.

The Tripuris moved from one place to another a lot before they settled down. So they must have picked up many languages too!

MANY DIALECTS

The official language of Tripura is *Bangla Bhasha* or Bengali. That's because for a long time it was a part of the Bengal Presidency. But there are many tribal languages that people speak here. One of the main languages is called Kokborok. This can be called the second official language of Tripura. Let's learn some phrases in this language.

Good morning =
Phung kaham

Good night =
Hor kaham

Very good =
Hamsukkha

Don't worry =
Tauanandi

Good
evening =
Sanja kaham

Sit down =
Achukdi

How are
you? =
Kaham de?

When did
you come? =
Nwng buphru
phaikha?

Thank
you =
Humbai

MATCH
THE MASTERS

Mishki and Pushka want to be sure they remember the words they have learnt. Can you help them by matching the English phrases to their Kokborok translations?

Don't worry	Humbai
Good evening	Kaham de?
Thank you	Sanja kaham
Very good	Tauanandi
How are you?	Phung kaham
Good morning	Hamsukkha

A peep into their life

Tripura looks very colourful. You did say there are many tribes in this state. The culture must also be very colourful, right?

The mix of tribal and classical customs is common to many other states in India. But let's not waste time. Let's see some customs and traditions that are unique to this tiny state.

MEET THE FOLK

There are close to twenty tribes that call Tripura home. Some of them have always lived in the hills. But many have migrated to India from across the border. Reang, Noatia, Uchai, Chaimal, Halam, Kuki, Garo, Mog, Chakma, Munda, Orang, Santal . . . Phew! The list goes on. Together, they all are simply known as Tripuris.

KHARCHI PUJA

The word *kharchi* literally means 'cleansing of sin'. During this festival, people pray to Tripura's fourteen main deities. Priests and devotees chant loudly as they carry these deities to the river Saidra. They bathe in the holy water and wash the idols. Then they decorate the idols and carry them back to the temple. During this festival, people believe that they are purifying the earth and cleansing themselves of any sin too!

DURGA PUJA

Like in Bengal, Durga Puja is possibly the most popular festival in Tripura. They pray to Goddess Durga for ten days. On the tenth day, in colourful and loud processions, the idol of Goddess Durga is immersed in the river or the sea. This festival is a grand celebration of good over evil.

ASHOKASHTAMI FESTIVAL

This festival is one that is celebrated with a grand fair that thousands of people flock to. Devotees take a dip in the holy water at a place called Unakoti. They pray to the deities, which are carved into the hillsides of the Unakoti hills. And finally, they celebrate with fun, food and feasts that all fairs are known for.

GARIA PUJA

This festival celebrates harvest. For seven days, at the beginning of the harvest season, tribal folk perform this puja praying for a good harvest. When that's done, they sing and dance and make merry, because how can any celebration be complete without all of that?

SUPER SANGRAI

Sangrai is a festival during which people of the Mog tribe believe that if they pray to a particular tree, their wish will be granted. The younger members of the tribe go from house to house carrying a sapling of a tree they believe grants wishes. There is a lot of singing and dancing during this festival.

BOAT RACE

This fun event isn't a religious festival. It's more a cultural one during which teams compete in a fun race held at the Rudrasagar Lake. They row as fast as they can in not-too-big canoe-like boats. There's a grand prize for the winners. Anyone from any tribe can take part. The spectators cheer wildly and great fun is had by all.

BIZU BOOM

This fun dance is the joy of the Chakma tribe. It marks the end of the year as per the Bengali calendar and the beginning of a new one. It's another reason to have fun. The dancers perform this fun dance to local folk beats on instruments like the *baajhi*, *hengrang* and *dhulak*.

LOVELY LEBANG

The Lebang dance is a part of a harvest celebration. Just before the rains come crashing down, the dancers catch an insect called *lebang*—a tiny creature that heralds the onset of the monsoon. The male dancers use bamboo chips as musical instruments and make a tapping, clapping sound. The women join the fun, waving colourful scarves and dancing in a circle.

GO GARIA!

In some tribal communities, Garia is the god of farming. After the hard work of sowing seeds is done, the farmers and their family celebrate by singing and dancing and praying to Garia for a good harvest.

HAI HAK HO

The Hai Hak dance is a speciality of the Halam tribe. This too is a harvest dance. Once the season of farming is over, the tribal folk collect for a grand prayer and dance during which they pray to Goddess Lakshmi, the goddess of wealth, for a bountiful harvest.

JHUM JOY

It's time to rest a while. The Tripuris do a dance called Jhum, which is an occasion for people to forget about work for a while and give themselves time to enjoy. It is meant to inspire people to work even harder when it's time to clear the fields for the next sowing season by giving them a well-deserved, fun break in advance.

HOZAGIRI

This dance is performed mainly by the women of the Reang tribe. While praying to Goddess Lakshmi, the dancers perform complicated steps. They stand atop an earthen pot while balancing a bottle on their head. A lamp is placed on or in the bottle. The dancers twist and bend, performing complex steps without dropping the bottle or the lamp.

GRAND GALAMUCHAMO

This dance is performed after a tiring harvesting season, when the farmers thank the gods for a good harvest. They wear traditional finery and sing and dance, celebrating their hard work.

MUSIC MANIA

The instruments of Tripura are quite unique. Most of them are made of simple wood, but the sounds they produce are incredible.

Sumui:
A small flute-like instrument

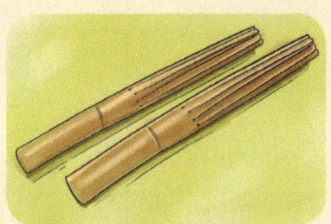

Lebang Lebangti:
A bamboo instrument that creates claps and twangs

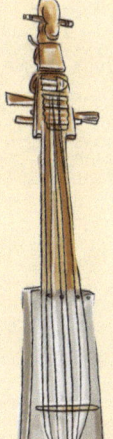

Chongpreng:
A guitar-like instrument made of hollow wood

Uakhrap:
A string instrument made from the trunk of a tree

Kham
A barrel-shaped drum made of goatskin

SHADOW PLAY

Mishki wants to set up her own band, so she's collecting musical instruments. Can you find the shadow of Mishki's guitar?

 A

 B

 C

 D

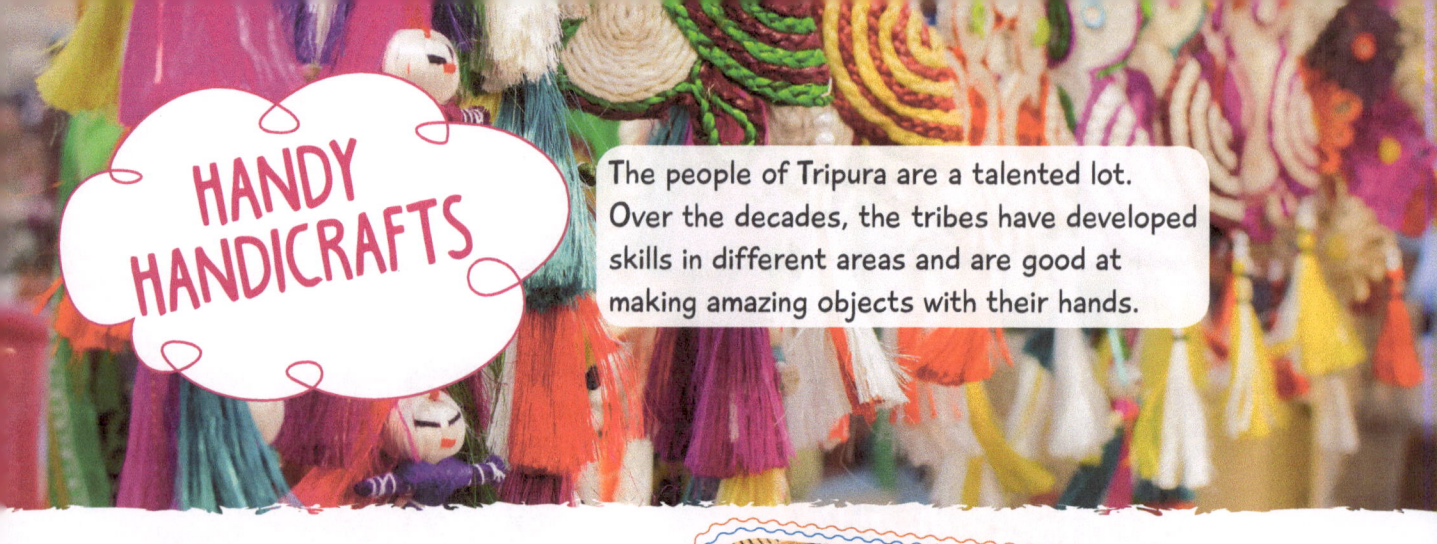

The people of Tripura are a talented lot. Over the decades, the tribes have developed skills in different areas and are good at making amazing objects with their hands.

BAMBOO MASTERPIECES

There are lots of bamboo trees in the forests of Tripura and people have been using it to make things for generations. They make beautiful mats, bags, lampshades and furniture, all of which is famous across the world.

AMAZING BASKETRY

Basket-making is a unique skill that the people of Tripura seem to be especially good at. There are baskets for different purposes—firewood baskets, baskets to carry dates, baskets for carrying crops, tea baskets and a whole lot more.

MAGICAL HANDLOOM

The Tripuris weave their own cloth, and what wonderful cloth it is! They use a loom called the lion loom that they have developed themselves. The cloth Tripura is best known for has bright stripes—both horizontal and vertical.

PATTERN PERFECT

Mishki is trying to weave a striped cloth like the people of Tripura do. Can you find two that are exactly alike?

A   B   C   D   E

There are four word searches here.
They each have some words about Tripura hidden in them.
Can you find all the hidden words?

DANCE DANCE

Can you find six dances from Tripura hidden here?

A	S	E	B	R	T	B	M	N	Y	O
A	S	D	J	H	U	M	G	F	Q	W
Z	X	C	V	B	N	M	A	S	D	F
G	A	L	A	M	U	C	H	A	M	O
A	S	D	F	G	H	J	K	L	Q	W
Z	X	H	A	I	H	A	K	H	O	Q
Q	W	E	R	T	Y	U	I	O	A	S
A	S	L	E	B	A	N	G	G	Q	W
Z	X	C	V	B	N	Q	B	I	Z	U
F	D	H	O	Z	A	G	I	R	I	A

WILDLIFE WOES

Can you find ten wild animals and birds from Tripura in this grid?

A	S	D	F	R	E	W	A	Z	X	I
A	L	E	O	P	A	R	D	Q	W	B
G	A	U	R	A	S	D	F	G	H	I
H	G	F	T	I	G	E	R	Z	X	S
Z	X	C	V	B	N	M	A	S	D	F
A	S	D	F	Q	G	A	Y	A	L	C
L	I	O	N	E	J	A	C	K	A	L
O	I	U	Y	T	R	E	W	Q	K	J
A	S	D	E	L	E	P	H	A	N	T
T	E	A	L	V	S	T	O	R	K	C

SPOT THEM ALL

Five of Tripura's main cities and five rivers are hidden in this grid. Find them all!

Z	X	A	G	A	R	T	A	L	A	Q
A	S	D	F	G	K	H	O	W	A	I
U	D	A	I	P	U	R	X	C	V	B
W	T	E	L	I	A	M	U	R	A	B
D	H	A	R	M	A	N	A	G	A	R
D	X	J	V	D	H	A	L	A	A	I
E	C	U	R	B	L	A	M	A	N	U
O	O	R	U	T	R	E	W	Q	A	Z
K	A	I	L	A	S	H	A	H	A	R

TRIBAL TRICKS

There are ten tribes from Tripura hiding in this word grid. Can you find them?

Q	S	D	R	T	H	G	M	O	G
A	R	E	A	N	G	L	O	I	T
S	D	N	O	A	T	I	A	D	G
S	A	N	T	A	L	K	J	H	G
Z	X	C	V	H	A	L	A	M	C
K	U	K	I	W	M	U	N	D	A
A	S	D	F	U	G	A	R	O	Q
L	K	J	H	G	F	D	S	A	Q
X	V	C	H	A	I	M	A	L	A
A	D	G	O	R	A	N	G	D	R

Bricks and stones

ECO-FRIENDLY

The traditional houses of the tribal folk in Tripura are eco-friendly. They are built using natural material. Different tribes may have slightly different features, but almost all the houses are made of cane, bamboo, mud and thatch. There are three main types of houses.

THE RIANG HOUSE

The house of the Riang tribe is an example of a typical Tripuri tribal home. Often built on a hill, the Riang house is usually a long rectangle. It has a front veranda, a back veranda and a biggish room in between. The house is usually built on stilts.

MUD HOUSES

The mud houses of Tripura are made entirely of mud, except for the roof that is made of thatch. The mud is heated and baked in the hot sun. These houses are seen more on the plains of Tripura.

BAMBOO, MUD AND TIN

And then there are those people, especially those living closer to cities, who mix all the materials to build houses. These houses are built by people who don't move from place to place, so their houses can be more permanent. The roofs and walls are made of tin. The inner walls are made of bamboo. Floors are often made of mud. It's a perfect combination.

Standing strong

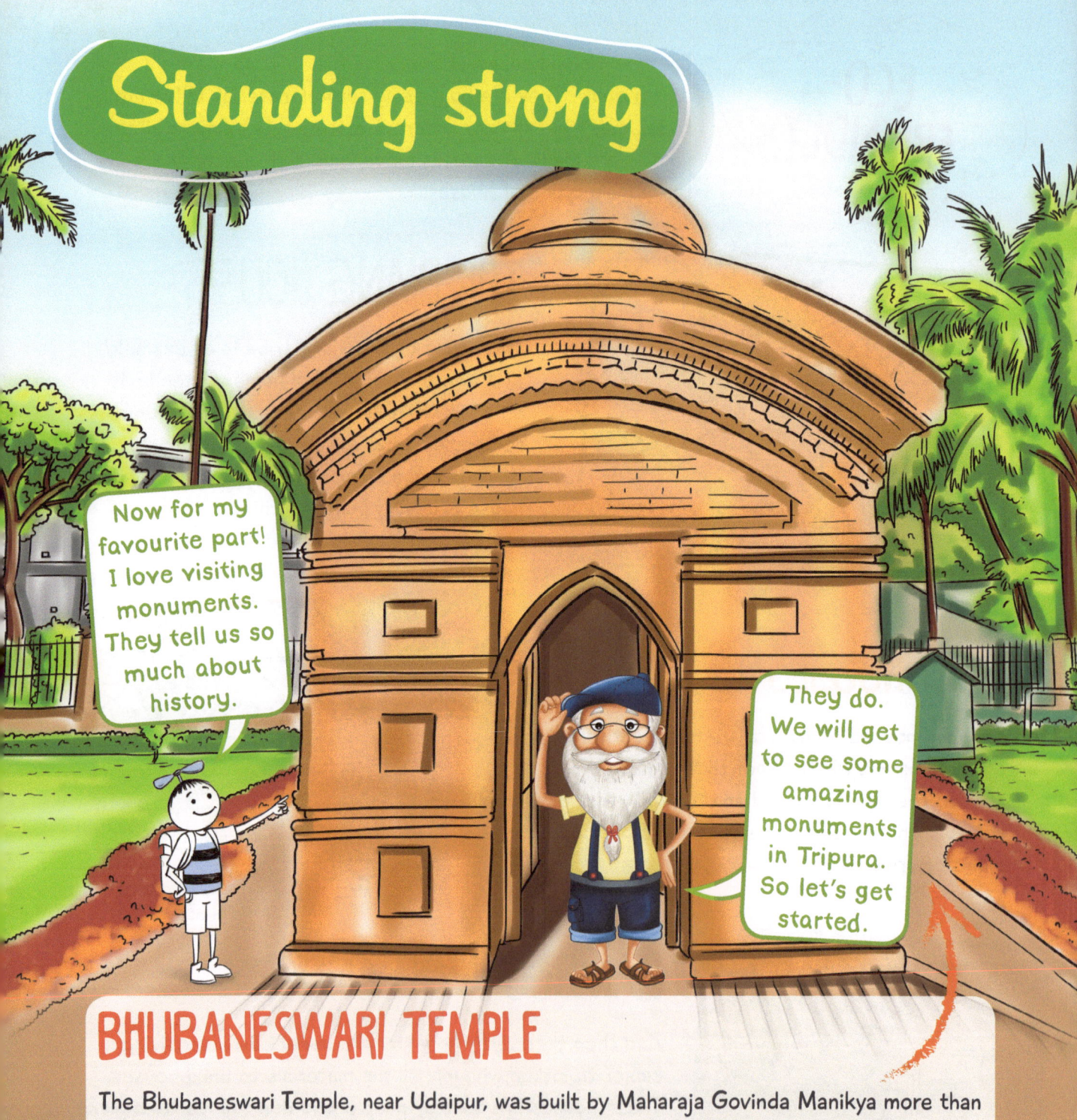

Now for my favourite part! I love visiting monuments. They tell us so much about history.

They do. We will get to see some amazing monuments in Tripura. So let's get started.

BHUBANESWARI TEMPLE

The Bhubaneswari Temple, near Udaipur, was built by Maharaja Govinda Manikya more than 300 years ago. It's a simple-looking temple but is of no less importance to its thousands of devotees. It became even more famous when the well-known poet Rabindranath Tagore wrote about it in his books.

THE CHATURDASHA TEMPLE

Tripura has fourteen deities that people pray devoutly to. The Chaturdasha Temple, near Agartala, was built to honour these deities. During the Kharchi Puja, thousands of devotees flock to this temple to offer prayers.

TRIPURA SUNDARI TEMPLE

This is an important temple with a rather scary story behind it. Sati was Lord Shiva's wife. She married him against the wishes of her father, who was so upset he insulted them both. Sati could not bear this and she died. Full with grief, Lord Shiva picked up the body of his beloved wife and danced the *Shiva Tandava*, also called the dance of destruction. As he danced, Sati's right foot landed where the Tripura Sundari Temple stands today! People come all over India to pray at this temple that is well-known as a Shakti peetha. Oooh! What a story!

KAMALASAGAR KALI TEMPLE

This lovely temple devoted to Goddess Kali stands next to the Kamalasagar Lake, and was constructed by Maharaja Dhanya Manikya more than 500 years ago. Located near Agartala, this charming temple draws thousands of devotees and tourists.

ANCIENT RUINS

There are some amazing ancient ruins in Tripura that tell us much about how people lived in ancient times.

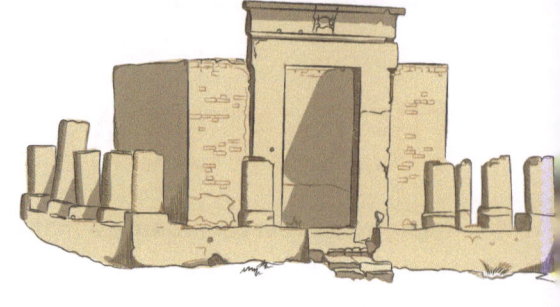

BUDDHIST RUINS AT BOXANAGAR

A while ago, some archaeologists discovered something at a place called Boxanagar that left them stunned. They found the ruins of what seemed to have once been a Buddhist monastery and settlement. There is a large building that suggests that at one time, maybe thousands of years ago, Buddhism might have prevailed in this region.

CHABIMURA ROCK CARVINGS

There's a steep mountain right in the middle of thick forests, where you come across a sight that is quite unbelievable. The rock carvings of various gods and goddesses like Shiva, Vishnu and Durga on a steep mountain wall can leave you spellbound. These are said to be more than 500 years old. You can imagine the skill of the people who must have carved these. To get there, you have to trek through some pretty dense forests.

DISCOVERING HISTORY

Excavations in this region unearthed ruins in a place called Pilak, which tell us that thousands of years ago many cultures lived here together. Archaeologists were delighted to find a huge collection of statues, seals, images and structures that seem to be both Buddhist and Hindu. The style of carving is similar to other pieces found in areas where the Pala and Gupta dynasties ruled. This is how historians get an idea of who ruled where, so many thousands of years ago.

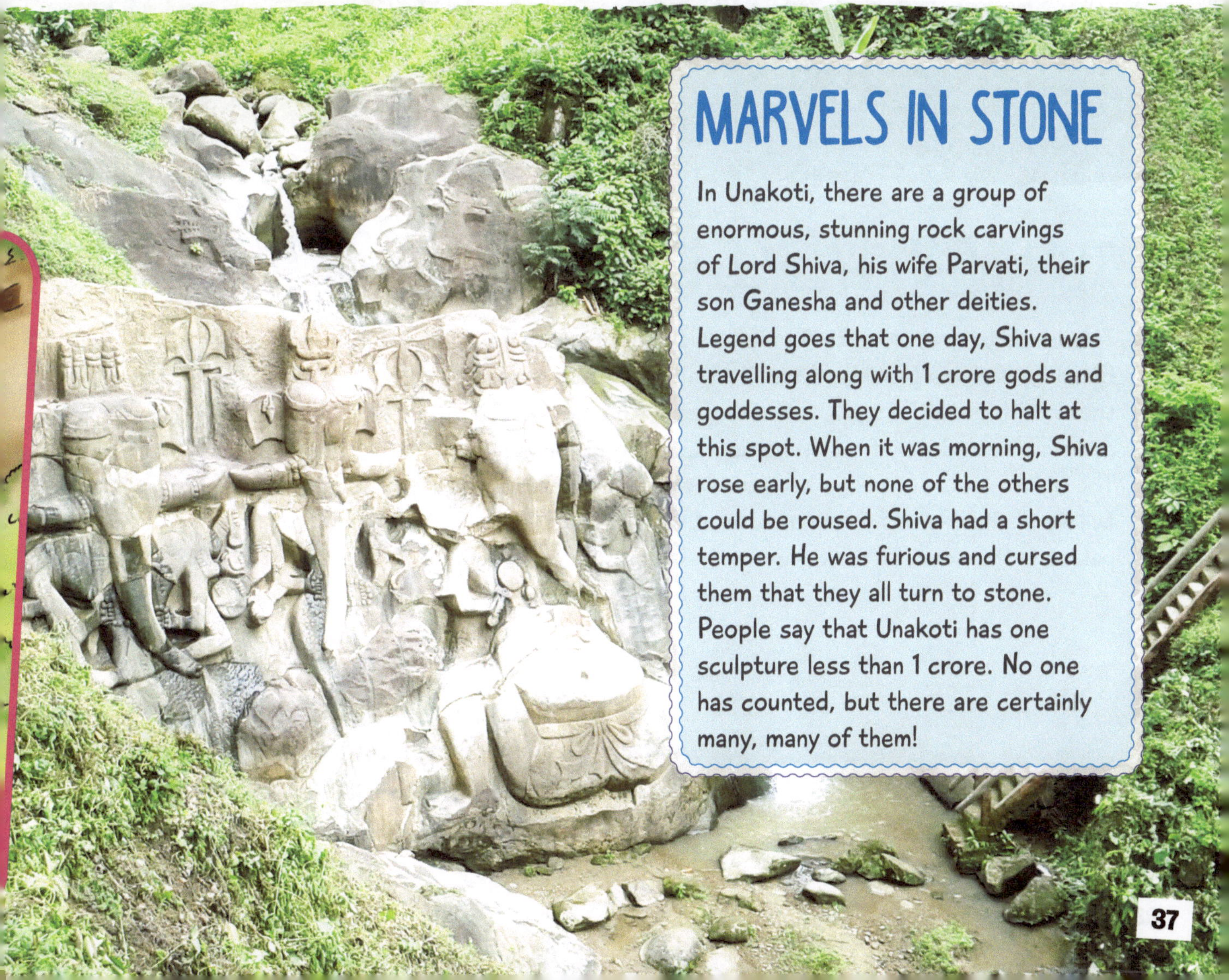

MARVELS IN STONE

In Unakoti, there are a group of enormous, stunning rock carvings of Lord Shiva, his wife Parvati, their son Ganesha and other deities. Legend goes that one day, Shiva was travelling along with 1 crore gods and goddesses. They decided to halt at this spot. When it was morning, Shiva rose early, but none of the others could be roused. Shiva had a short temper. He was furious and cursed them that they all turn to stone. People say that Unakoti has one sculpture less than 1 crore. No one has counted, but there are certainly many, many of them!

ROYAL SPLENDOUR

With nearly 200 Maharajas having ruled Tripura over the centuries, there are bound to be some lovely palaces. Let's go a peek at some of them.

KUNJABAN PALACE

This lovely palace, close to Agartala, was built by Maharaja Birendra Kishore Manikya. Like all royalty, he made sure there were beautiful gardens for his family to enjoy. There are even some lovely fruit orchards within the grounds. The palace walls and pillars have detailed carvings all over, telling us that he was a man of refined taste. Now the palace is the home of the governor of Tripura.

THE WATER PALACE

The name of this palace is Neermahal, which means water palace. This palace was built by Maharaja Bir Bikram Kishore Manikya Bahadur in the middle of Lake Rudrasagar. When you see the minarets, you know he was obviously quite inspired with Mughal architecture.

RHYME TIME

Mishki has made up a poem about royal life.
Can you help her complete it?

Kings and queens are so lucky
They live in palaces so grand
They're welcomed everywhere they go
With a big, musical _____

But sometimes I wonder if I'd rather be
Just a simple girl
So I can go wherever I want
In the big, exciting _____

Working hard

There's no doubt that it's a great place. But to live here means you will have to find an occupation too! So let's see what people here do for a living.

Tripura seems like a really cool place to live.

FARMER, FARMER, WHAT DO YOU GROW?

More than half the people of Tripura are involved in the farming business—even though most of the land isn't quite suitable for agriculture, because of hills and forests. Farmers still manage to produce quite a lot of crops. Almost all the farms are rice-producing. But farmers also work hard to grow potatoes, sugarcane, jute and various pulses. You'll see entire families pitching in.

SOMETHING FISHY

Pisciculture, or breeding fish, is another important occupation that many people are involved in. Thanks to the many lakes and rivers, fish farmers breed fish that they sell on a large scale. It not only gives people a means of livelihood, but also helps with food supply.

RUBBER MANIA

Did you know that Tripura is the second larger producer of rubber in India? Wow! There are many rubber plantations in Tripura that keep many people fully occupied. The rubber produced here is used to make many things, like pipes, flooring, medical gloves, belts, tyres and a whole lot more.

TIME FOR TEA

The climate of Tripura makes it perfect for people to grow tea. There are more than fifty large tea plantations and many more small tea growers. There are lots of people who work in these, either as tea-pickers or in the business of processing, packing and selling the tea grown here.

GAS STORIES

Natural gas, a very important source of energy, is found deep underground in rock formations. Tripura has many reservoirs of natural gas underneath its land. There are many companies that have set up massive refineries to get this gas out and convert it for use in homes, offices and factories. Many people work hard in these refineries to make this natural gas available to us.

TOURIST TALK

The government is encouraging tourists to come to Tripura. This has resulted in a growing tourist industry. This means more hotels, more restaurants, more shops and more airlines. All of this is giving people more options in occupation. Which is why a fairly large number of people work in this industry.

WOOD WORKERS

The large number of forests in Tripura have many strong and useful trees like sal, garjan, teak and gamar. Felling these trees and converting them into useful products is also an occupation that provides people with employment.

CRAFTING THINGS OF BEAUTY

As we've seen, the handicrafts of Tripura are famous. There are many craftsmen who, for generations, have been working hard to weave amazing cloth, carve wood to make furniture and weave baskets and other objects with bamboo. These are not large businesses, but there are many people engaged in them.

Did you know?
You'll see that many people from the north-eastern states of India have similar skills.

MATCH THE WORDS

Can you draw a line to match the words in the top row with the words in the bottom row?

| Wood | Weave | Tourist | Natural gas | Tea | Pisciculture |

| Lake | Plantation | Cloth | Underground | Hotel | Furniture |

Yum yum yum

I am more than ready for our food journey now, Daadu.

You are always ready for our food trip. So I won't make you wait another minute. Let's explore some of Tripura's fabulous food.

NICE AND HEALTHY

Tripura's traditional cuisine is called Mui Borok by its people. You'll find that the food is inspired by its next-door neighbour Bangladesh. There's also a touch of China in some of its food, probably because long ago, many tribes made their way here from China. One thing really great about Mui Borok cuisine is that the Tripuris don't use too much oil. So the food is quite healthy.

BERMA BONANZA

Berma is an ingredient that you'll find in many dishes in Tripura. This is a dried and fermented fish called *puti* that is stored and kept ready for use. When it's time to cook, it is added to many dishes, making the flavour unique and typically Tripuri.

DRINK UP!

Most adults in Tripura love to drink a traditional drink made of rice, bamboo and sometimes papaya and meat! They ferment rice in water and make a drink called chauk. They enjoy it during festivals, weddings and other celebrations. Apong, muya and awandru are other drinks they love to have. Not everybody's cup of tea, but they love it for sure.

GO FOR GUDOK

This lovely traditional dish used to be made by stuffing bamboo pipes with vegetables and meat, and cooking it over a slow fire. But now, this particular kind of bamboo isn't available very easily so people cook it in pans—something that's convenient but loses out on the yummy flavour that bamboo brings.

KOSOI BWTWI

This hot favourite of the Tripuris is made of beans and berma. It's a healthy dish that people enjoy having with rice.

KOTHALOR CHAKOI

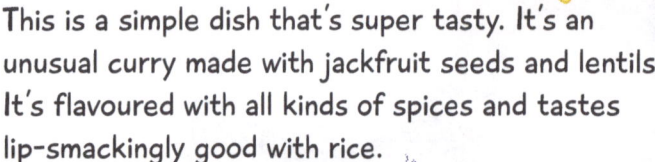

This is a simple dish that's super tasty. It's an unusual curry made with jackfruit seeds and lentils. It's flavoured with all kinds of spices and tastes lip-smackingly good with rice.

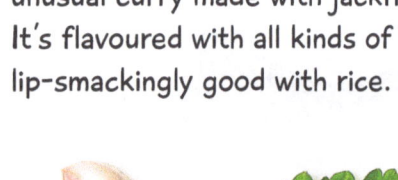

WAHAN MOSDENG

This meaty dish is a hot favourite of local people. It's a glorious blend of meat, onions and spices. It's a dry dish that people have either as a starter or as a main course. Either way, they love it!

PANCH PHORON TARKARI

Aha! Taste this and you feel like you are in Bengal. Right from the name of the dish to its taste, it smacks of Bengali cuisine. Panch phoron refers to a mix of five different spices. This dish is made with different vegetables. It tastes best with puris or parathas.

BHANGUI

This delicious rice dish is made with a lot of love and care. Cooks first dry the rice in the sun. Then they cook it with ghee, onion and ginger. It's then boiled in a banana leaf and served piping hot along with various curries that the state is famous for.

MOSDENG SERMA

This is a tangy, spicy, mouth-watering chutney that adds zing to any meal. Tripuris grind tomato, berma, chillies and garlic to make this yummy paste.

CAKE, ANYONE?

The people of Tripura get really creative when it comes to cake. There are many types of local cakes that they make, using the most unusual ingredients, and no celebration is ever complete without one of these. Guria is one such cake made with sticky rice and jaggery.

YUMMY CROSSWORD

Solve this picture crossword

48

SPOT THE
DIFFERENCES

Pushka has gone vegetable shopping. There are ten differences in the two pictures of the Farmers' Market he's visited. Can you find them?

What to wear?

Now it's MY favourite part. I love seeing local clothes. Are the costumes of Tripura unusual, Daadu?

You will soon find out. Every state has clothes best suited to its local climate and materials. Tripura is no different. Come, let's explore.

LIKE ITS SIX SISTERS

Though the Tripuris have their own traditional costumes, many of these are similar to the tribal costumes in the other six states that are its sisters in the North-east. The pattern of Tripura fabric is quite unique, though.

FEMALE FASHION

The women wear a sarong-like outfit. The lower part is called a *rignai*. The blouse is called *risa* and *rikutu*. In the olden days, women would weave these themselves.

THEIR OWN PATTERNS

Every clan or tribe used to have their own unique rignai patterns. But now, with inter-tribal marriages, there are newer patterns emerging.

People say that Subrai Raja, one of Tripura's kings, had nearly 250 wives. And guess how he chose his wives? Whenever a woman created a new rignai design, he would make her his bride. So thanks to him, more than 250 rignai patterns became popular in Tripura in the ancient times.

MALE STYLE

For their everyday work, men typically wear something that's very convenient. They wear a simple half-lungi cloth called *rikutu gamcha*. They team this with a home-woven shirt called *kubai*. During festivals, they wear brightly coloured jackets too!

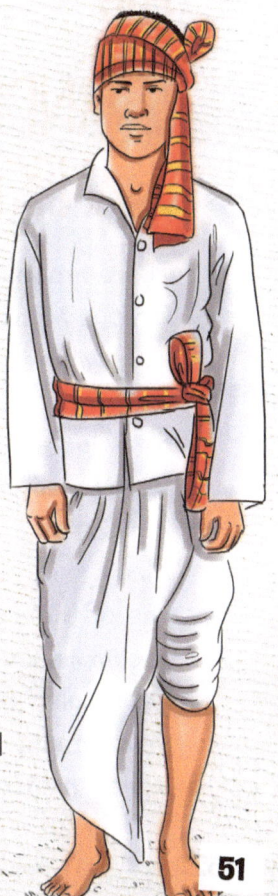

JEWELLERY JOY!

Women in Tripura love their jewellery and for any occasion, they adorn themselves with beads, coins and other kinds of exotic jewellery. Now this tribal jewellery has become famous across India and tourists love buying it.

Autograph, please?

The Tripuris seem to be a creative people. There must be some amazing achievers, right?

You're right! There are some people in Tripura who have achieved a lot. Some of them have become very famous too, and while others may not be that well known, their achievements are just as amazing.

MAHARAJA BIR CHANDRA MANIKYA

There are many famous Manikya kings who have done a lot for Tripura. But Maharaja Bir Chandra Manikya is one of the more accomplished ones. Not only was he a great ruler, but he was also a poet, scholar, photographer and educationist. So many achievements! Isn't that amazing?

SACHIN DEV BURMAN

Known affectionately as SD, this great musician and singer was originally a member of a Tripura royal family. He started his career composing music for Bengali films, but later moved to Hindi films as well. He soon became one of India's best-known composers and his style of music was very unique and very, very popular even today.

MAHARANI TULSIBATI

She was a revolutionary queen whose full name was Radha Kishore Manikya. Though she was born a simple peasant girl, she became a famous queen when she married into the royal family. She did a lot to promote women's education. The first girls' school in Tripura is named after her.

SOMDEV DEVVARMAN

He is a tennis player from Tripura who competed in international tennis tournaments. He also won the gold medal in the 2010 Commonwealth Games and the 2010 Asian Games.

DIPA KARMAKAR

This brilliant athlete was the first Indian female gymnast to compete in the Olympics. Though she didn't win a medal in the Olympics, standing fourth, she is the pride of Tripura. She was awarded the Padma Shri by the Indian government for her brilliance in her field.

RAHUL DEV BURMAN

This dynamic musician was the son of SD Burman. He was fondly called Pancham. Though he didn't live in Tripura, nor was he born there, his roots were from Tripura. He brought a whole new style of music into Hindi cinema that became very popular.

Once upon a time . . .

Daadu, I would like to become a writer when I grow up. And I want to hear stories from around the world so that I get inspired.

Well, there are some lovely folk tales from Tripura that can inspire you. I can tell you one right away!

THE FLOWER OF HEAVEN

There was a young man called Sbapan who lived in a small village in Tripura. He had a young and pretty wife named Hutah, whom he loved very much. The young couple was happy together.

It was the season of harvesting. Sbapan was helping Hutah's father on the field. After a hard day of work, he, along with Hutah set off on the long walk home to their own village, a few miles away.

To get home, they had to walk through a small forest. They used the same path everyday and were quite used to it. They were walking along when suddenly Hutah stopped.

'Oh! What a lovely fragrance!' she exclaimed. 'Where is it coming from?'

Sbapan looked around. He was more familiar with the forest than his wife was, for he had earned his living cutting trees when he was younger. He spotted the flower.

'That is the fragrance of the Kherengbar flower,' he explained. 'Look, there it is.' And he pointed to a beautiful flower.

Hutah looked at the flower and gasped. She had never seen such a beautiful flower in her life.

'Oh! What a gorgeous flower! I must have it!' she exclaimed. 'Please, can you pick it for me? I want to put it in my hair.'

'No, Hutah, you cannot put that flower in your hair. It is the flower of heaven. It harms us humans' Sbapan explained. 'An angel brought it to earth and made it grow on a tree. That is why it grows on a tree trunk and never on soil,' he added.

'I don't care. I want it.' Hutah was adamant. 'And besides, how can a flower harm us?'

'Well, I don't know anyone to whom it has happened, but I've heard that if this flower is put into anyone's hair, then the person who picked it will turn into a *huluk*.'

A huluk is a type of gibbon monkey. Hutah found the idea hilarious.

'That's rubbish. I want the flower RIGHT NOW!' she said, and stamped her foot angrily.

Now Sbapan loved his wife very much. He simply could not refuse. He climbed the tree and plucked the flower.

'Here it is' he said, handing the lovely flower to Hutah. 'But please don't put it in your hair,' he warned her.

As soon as Hutah had the lovely flower in her hand, she couldn't control herself. She put it in her hair at once, even as Sbapan tried to stop her.

'I don't believe in old wives' tales,' she scoffed.

And suddenly, even as she tucked the flower behind her ear, something strange began to happen. Sbapan's hands began to grow claws and they got stuck to the branch of the tree. His features began to change. And soon he had turned into a huluk.

'Oh, husband!' Hutah cried, distraught. 'What have I done!!! How can I turn you back into a human?'

Sbapan tried to call out Hutah's name, but the only sound he could make was 'Huk huk hutah.'

Ever since, gibbons, they say, make the sound 'huk huk hutah.' Even the gods were sorry to see poor Sbapan's condition. Upset with the Kherengbar flower, they took away its lovely fragrance so that it wouldn't tempt anyone ever again.

TRAVEL DIARY

Have you enjoyed this trip to Tripura with your friends Mishki and Pushka—and, of course, with Daadu Dolma?

Now you can make your own Tripura diary. And if you ever visit Tripura, make sure you take pictures and put them in the photo box.

The first place I would visit in Tripura:

_____

If I could perform one of the folk dances, I would perform:

_____

The one dish I am definitely going to eat:

_____

The monument I think is the most interesting:

_____

The one famous person from Tripura I would love to meet:

_____

I think the most interesting historical figure from Tripura is:

_____

The festival from Tripura that I think is the most fun:

_____

The five words that I think describe Tripura the best are:

_____

_____

_____

_____

_____

My Tripura memories:

ANSWERS

Page 9 **LEOPARD SPOTTING**

A and D are twins.

Page 11 **FARM MAZE**

Page 13 **HIDDEN WORDS**

Here are some of words you can form: art, rag, rat, tag, tar, altar, lag, at, a, alt

Page 21 **MATCH THE MASTERS**

Don't worry—Tauanandi; Good evening—Sanja kaham; Thank you—Humbai; Very good—Humsukkha; How are you?—Kaham de?; Good morning—Phung kaham

Page 27 **SHADOW PLAY**

D is the correct shadow.

Page 29 **PATTERN PERFECT**

A and D are exactly alike.

Page 30 **WORD SEARCH WONDER**

DANCE DANCE

WILDLIFE WOES

SPOT THEM ALL

TRIBAL TRICKS

Page 39 **RHYME TIME**
band, world

Page 43 **MATCH THE WORDS**

Wood—Furniture; Weave—Cloth; Tourist—Hotel; Natural gas—Underground; Tea—Plantation; Pisciculture—Lake

Page 48 **YUMMY CROSSWORD**

Page 49 **SPOT THE DIFFERENCES**